The Book of Life
Vol. III
O.E. Simon

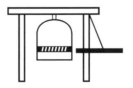

Golden Bell Publishing House Inc.

1st Edition published in 2000

Illustrations by James Vensel and Alex Fong
Jacket Painting by Alex Fong
Jacket Design by Ken Laninga

Canadian Cataloguing in Publication Data:

Simon, O.E. (Olaf Emil), 1929 -
        Book of Life
Poems.
ISBN 0-9683504-3-7

        I.Title.
PS8587.I34B64 1999   C811'.54   C99-900457-3
PR9199.3.S5193B64 1999

Published by

Golden Bell Publishing House Inc.
Grand Forks, B.C. VOH IHO
Canada
www.goldenbellhouse.com
info@goldenbellhouse.com
Printed In Canada

Book of Life
Vol. III
of
The Quadriga

About the Author

Born in Europe, O.E. Simon was exposed to both the pre war and the World War II years, seeing man at his worst, most evil, most cruel and at his best, people helping others under the most inhumane conditions. It was perhaps this preparation that made him even more equipped to become the poet and novelist that he is today. After the war, he educated himself and was the recipient of his country's national literary award for his Durnburger Hexameter. Still unable to find fulfilment for his idealism, he chose to leave Europe and seek out a new country.

In North America, he has found fulfilment and success as a poet and novelist and also as a teacher. Becoming the spiritual leader of the Neo Ch'an Buddhist Temple (a reformed Buddhism which believes in God) has enabled him to fulfill a lifelong ambition, namely to unite all religions which believe in one creator, under one roof of worship for the sake of peace and for the future of mankind on this earth.

About the Artists:

James Vensel originally illustrated the first two volumes of The Quadriga in the 1970's, having a wonderful sensitivity for understanding precisely what the author was trying to say. He is now living on Vancouver Island and is retired enjoying the inspiration and peace of the surroundings.

Alex Fong is a young artist living in British Columbia and becoming well known for his beautiful interpretations combining the sensitivity of his Chinese heritage with international topics, lending always a special, spiritual quality to his work.

Book of Life

Table of Contents

The Citizen of All

Oh yes, my Lord, thy name has raised its veil into the heights of heaven, has freed the shores for many ships to land and, yes, it was a struggle often with the unknown as we searched out to walk new lands which others held so unbeknown to us before we came. Yes, most of us fled other shores to reach a better one which offered space, new hope, if courage stayed with us. But as we fought and stumbled through this land, our errors went along with us until we forged for reason. And yes, we started new. We had the courage to begin to change our ways return to you, that glorious spirit, hallowed by thy name with which we shaped decrees, enshrined our laws into the vellum best to shield, to uplift all before a holy shrine, to make man free, but show him in these scripts from whence this action grew that men, all men, remain thus sovereign of anything which strangles tolerance, the string with which the heavens hold the breath of faith. Under such God we raised our flag and freed the heavens wide; so far, in fact, that any faith may share into our space. And as we are of many, so we are of one, united, not alone but with the many different colours that our faces show when they reflect from our shining waters, lakes and streams as they flow on in time, while our sun, the sun which touches our shores, remembers that this space, these hallowed, deep green meadows, gilded plains of our land will answer our past. We will again, and yes again, return to our roots as we describe our tries, recalling all the names who struggled on to keep us one, who carry us to battlefields on which we kneel with our children not yet born, reflect in spirit and in deed. To close and distant graves we pass our tears to last forever. As our present joys demand recall, we shall become of them once more, allowing us to walk so tall that our spirits touch their souls in heaven. Who then can dwarf our mountains' heights, erase their glittering icefields high up yonder in the azure domed sky, the same Elysium in which our eagles stray unhindered still, untouched by hostile spirits as we breathe? Who yet will dare to plant the seed of hate before we plow our fields? Who taunts and agitates our souls away from peace which lifts up high exalting thus itself within the crimson sunrise, splendorous rays, marking so well our peaceful sky? And who will dare to dim the many stars our colours fly when foes attempt to tear its seams? Only our people can dispute it all or raise this challenge higher up as yet toward the stars, these gleaming suns which scintillate of time, unprecedented ages, yet to come.

And yes, my people, if nothing else is being said of you, we claim to have not lost one spirit of this clan, the citizen of all, the one we call -

" American."

Christina's Lake

There dwells a lake like never has another.
Its secret holds of wonders little known.
And if you walk and rest and do not bother
and seek the night when moonbeams roam

you'll hear a voice so clear and fond, a treasure
within the sleeping waves to come awake.
Then if you hold one breath for silent measure
you'll know you touched Christina's lake.

The maid has long since sent enchantments calling,
when nights were filled with blossoms' bliss.
When distant sunlight touches stars while falling,
she's known to send a secret kiss.

The story holds a tempting call for others
who wander nights along to lure from wake
of waves her warming song to lovers,
from past to present in her lake.

It is her song which holds all pleasures quiet.
It knows of love and all its trends.
So if you have a sweetheart, you should try it
before the blossom falling ends.

She sings about an eagle's falling feather
and tells that if you catch one drifting high
you will in love and life remain together
in happiness until you die.

But if you tell and boast and lead the crowds near
and let them shout, and rage and scream,
you would at once disturb the silence out here.
Her song would end, just while you dream.

There dwells a lake like never has another.
It's filled with love of years gone by.
So if you do come here, be quiet rather
and keep this secret as do I.

11

To Dustin..

(This poem was dedicated to Dustin Hoffman
when the author met him in 1970)

Dust-like collapses the mountain
Under the earthquake's thunderous power
Sending out fear for life and for love,
Though sunlight shall rise like the silvery fountain
Inside of your soul to master the hour
Not to forget the blue sky above.

A Woman's Worth

A woman's worth like rise and fall
engraves what mankind gained in ages:
it lingers in the spirit of us all
or drives us back to empty cages.

'Tis how she thinks and how she talks
and with the pride she quiet hides,
and, sometimes, even how she walks
being a mother or a bride;
but most of all the things,
it is her manners - not her rings.

Trespassing

Strayed and placed away from heaven
midst the grass turned brown and dry,
found my heart a silent lesson
that the spirits never die.

Here to go and tread on prayers
long since gone and little known,
do they rest in formal layers
far beneath the heavens, thrown.

Rain and sun and ice are passing
as the mansion dwells in pleasure
without meaning as if nothing
would reveal the sleeping treasure.

Here to go and here to visit
called a voice from high above
that all wonders circle with it
if the heart is full of love.

Soon forgotten and plowed under
but remaining in some souls
for tomorrow's pleasant wonder
of our never changing roles.

Rest these sisters in their prayers,
in the minds of those alone
who alike forgotten sayers
were betrayed by distant Rome.

While You Sleep

Should my loving eyes
touch the willows by the creek,
where the stork still flies
will I kiss you while you sleep.

But comes autumn's time
when the coloured leaves must fall,
where you just were mine,
let the snow cover it all.

Love, my heart, too sweet
lies the purple snow today;
though I must not weep,
I will not forget to pray.

Where I kneel or stand,
where my tears still kiss the snow,
on you, sleeping land,
shall my love and sorrow flow.

Curse of the Gods

(Excerpt from the novel Curse of the Gods)

Out of storm and rain and snow
wound a train through Russia's past,
like a ghost which cannot go
pulling what its time had cast.

Come has what the rain had swept,
what he'd twisted into knots:
all the tears which still unwept
held the curses of the gods.

Time and time the hours turned
till a million coloured dots
grew upon what once was burned
by the curses of the gods.

Gone is what the thunder brought,
what he left for passers-by:
armies crushed by men who fought
never knowing they would die.

Out of storm and rain and snow
wound a train with captured slaves;
and the ghost that would not go
rose above a million graves.

Now the sun is setting low
'gainst the sky of Russia's past,
like a ghost which cannot go,
like a ghost which cannot last.

My Soldier

(Excerpt from the novel Curse of the Gods)

All the songbirds are still sleeping
and the grass is breathing low,
and the flowers are still weeping
'cause my soldier had to go.

But then comes the time to kiss you
and then comes the time to know
that your Russia, soldier, called you
back to where I cannot go.

Soon the winter makes his calling
and the year has passed us by.
Snowflakes drift and snowflakes falling
do not tell me why, oh why.

But then comes the time to kiss you
and then comes the time to know
that your Russia, soldier, called you
back to where I cannot go.

I have waited many hours
and you have not come to me,
though the blood red, blooming flowers
joyful talk of victory.

But then comes the time to kiss you
and then comes the time to know
that your Russia, soldier, called you
back to where I cannot go.

23

The Ghostly Rider

The morning wept on dew drenched meadows:
the leaves, their fragile stems reached high.
My horse's hooves like fleeing shadows
were flying by, were flying by.

Should you once see this fleeing rider
don't break a rose or hurl a curse:
a shadow's happiness will neither
be of the heavens or of earth.

'Tis where the morning greets my love
and where the silver willow tree
embraces earth and sky above
that makes this early day break free,
break free with joy to sing and see
the ghostly rider leaving me.

JIM VENSEL 97

Life's Circle

Prolonging the sunset is the reflection
engraving the breath of the day
above the emerald waters -
carving the hours towards the past
eternally slow - while life's
circle is trying to last.

The Painter

(dedicated to Duncan McKinnon Crockford 1976)

The empty canvas looked betrayed
against my friend, a painting man,
while high above the sky broke blue,
and when his eyes caught the portrait
it was his brush which slowly then
began to dream and flew and flew.

A river curved before my eyes
and on its shores he raised a tree
with brushstrokes strong to please the base.
Then soon the fairy distant flies
out from nowhere to frolic me,
to wander still from place to place.

And mountains grew and sunlight touched
a harvest scene, a falling leaf,
and then a stem, a flower broke
under his hand; just while I watched
a smile of his announced his grief
and one small tear his final stroke.

A man came by, he laughed and paid,
he took away his world and mine;
just praised his famous painting hand.
The night set in, although I stayed
to be once more within the shrine
of God's wide world beside my friend.

The night was deep and dark and true -
there was no moon but from afar
a starburst woke the sleeping sky
as if creation started new
a star within another star
and never asked to where and why.

Highways Above

So briskly, so silent, so filled with soft rays
surrounded by spirits of all that is well,
aloft with the soul of glorious days
so smilingly warm as tears only tell,
now walking the heavens on earth, if you will.

For all that we see are dwindling shadows
and roads which shall lead to highways above.
Beneath are our dreams of silver green meadows
just crowning the wandering moments of love.

And therefore you people and friends of my time,
let's praise any moment our hearts cannot hold
in song or in word of laughter and wine
and do not forget that suffering told
as you walk the earth while the heavens are mine.

For all that we see are dwindling shadows
and roads which shall lead to highways above.
Beneath are our dreams of silver green meadows
still crowning the wandering moments of love.

The Seven Wonders
of the Ancient World

The pyramids first, which in Egypt were laid;
next Babylon's garden for Amytis made;
then Mousolos' tomb of affection and guilt;
fourth, the Temple of Dian in Ephesus built;
the Colossus of Rhodes, cast in brass to the sun;
sixth, Jupiter's statue by Phidias done;
the Pharos, lighthouse of Egypt comes last, we are told,
if not the Palace of Cyrus, cemented with gold;
and least but not last, to remind us all,
they never included the Great Chinese Wall.

Freedom

I have passed the silent rivers,
sat on beaches free of men,
and have stalked a thousand paths
and still climbed the mountain then.

But when high in wing soared regions
my emotions feel the sun,
when beneath me silv'ry clouds drift,
do I know that I have won.

Sweeping on the edge of heaven
has my eager heartbeat dwelt
and amidst the twirling sunrays
with the praying angels knelt.

Up and downward like the eagle
swiftly felt monotony,
falling, falling from the aether
into earthly botany

sank my craft in giant spirals
here and there and then
back from godlike, golden heaven
towards the sphere of mortal men.

Now to see him where I left him
on the earth where he'd begun,
will I raise his holy spirit
'long the contrails to the sun.

Will I sing and praise the wonder
which the earthbound world not shows
having flown the far blue yonder
with a freedom no one knows.

In Vain

(*Excerpt from Curse of the Gods*)

Mankind derives from love alone
and loyalty bestows its reign;
but love of want becomes a throne
which proves all love to be in vain.

And what you gained since you began,
a glorious future promised new,
will double for the wealthy man
but prove to be a lie to you.

You lose your country for some gold
and see and hear what is to come;
but what they plan remains untold
and soon you wish your deed undone.

Stay with your country's glowing stars
but lend your neighbour any hand:
beware the war of all the wars
in which the traitor rules your land.

No Final Judgements

If I walk the distant meadow
or I rush the crowded streets,
we'll remain without each other
with a heart that never beats.

If you travel high on horseback
follow up a river's strand,
we'll remain without each other
if we lend no helping hand.

Thus, to make a world together
let us do what no one can;
no more hate for one another
mother, child or fellow man.

If a final war is coming
all that man has done is shed,
all that God has made to love in
will be doomed and will be dead.

In the end of all ambitions
have they failed to save this run:
since there are no final judgements
in a war that can't be won.

Let My People Go

(excerpt from the novel Curse of the Gods)

The snow will drift no more for me.
No golden dawn proclaims to reign
while all the sunlight glows to red
because too many have been slain.

I left my family behind,
my birthplace: all alone, in vain
I try. The lost I cannot find
because too many have been slain.

When once the snow will speak to thee,
to where my frozen body fell,
my smiling lips will silently
sing through the night to tell.

Oh let my people be.
Oh world with all your space,
a million stars to glow,
oh Lord, we ask your grace
to let my people go.

The Battle Hymn of Kursk

(excerpt from the novel Curse of the Gods)

Near Savidovka village there lies an unknown grave
and in the summer's cooling night
a song goes through the trees
of bygone battle's oversight.
In words, it sounds like these:
> Leave me no wreath and waste no word
> when you rebuild this land.
> Let far away my love be heard
> within the shifting sand.
> And where the shadow forest lies,
> in autumn leaves of falling gold,
> had echoed once a battle hymn
> to Russian sons some young, and some too old:
> to hold, to hold, for Russia's sake,
> > to hold, to hold, to hold.

Near Savidovka village there's still an unknown grave
where in the winter silver lined
this land will rest in peace
with all the memories behind.
In words, they sound like these:
> Leave me no tear but sing this song
> when you rebuild this land.
> Walk far away my girl, along,
> and dance and raise your hand
> until the balalaika sings
> of stories which are still untold,
> how we had sung this battle hymn
> for Russian sons, some young, and some too old:
> to hold, to hold, for Russia's sake,
> > to hold, to hold, to hold.

43

Brother Don

O, flow on you quiet river
pass by me for evermore,
so if lonesome I can never
be without your smiling shore.

Brother Don and Volga mother,
Sister Lena, rivers great,
mighty Amur, distant father
of the country's eastern gate.

O, flow on in rage and weather,
sing along my rivers be
with your never ending treasures
our whole eternity.

Time has left what it had started,
our friends have long since gone;
if the whole wide world has parted
we still have you, river Don.

If in iron held or prison,
if betrayed by our own,
raise the signs which we have given
the red colours to be flown.

Shalom to You, My Love..

(excerpt from the novel Shalom)

You stand now where I once walked,
above the deeply frozen snow:
the thousand prayers I have talked
            with nowhere left to go.
Now, since you're gone,
I'm all alone.
Without your fears,
I still find tears
            for our song.
Into the wind, I breathed your name
and with the moon I left your face:
our silent wishes never came
for all that we embraced.

            Shalom, to you my love,
            this quiet heart shall pray.
            Shalom to you, oh God
            help us to find the way.
            How slow to ear and eye at all
            do many tears still have to fall
            until the warming summer sun
            will bless the hope which now has gone.
            'Til I find you, 'til I find you,
            shalom, shalom, shalom.

Melting snow has kissed the land,
a million tears smile back at you
and where your lips have no command
is sunlight breaking through.
But since you're gone
            I'm all alone.
Without your heart
I cannot start
another song.
But when the leaves begin to fall
against an early sunset's glow,
shall I still wait until you call
my name amidst the snow.

47

Jim Vensel 97

One Sacred Word, My Wife

(excerpt from the novel Shalom)

With birches dressed more white than green
the molten snow has cried
itself into the wounded soil - oh gleam
of hope, it's still untied
beneath the quiet window sill
to bring, to give, to love
to wait no longer still.

With winter gone, I seek your lips
but nowhere you're around.
The icicle which broke and drips
now thawed my voice to sound
if sun, if snow, if rain,
I must, I must, I must
find you once more again.

Oh Russia, show a gentle heart,
thou aren't too great to cry.
If once you break this love apart
within your soil shall lie
a buried love to glow.
One sacred word, my 'wife',
shall linger in your snow.

Brothers Both

(excerpt from the novel Shalom)

Blow gentle winds, blow gentle on this hill.
Whether the night lays on its velvet cloth
or if the sunlight touches - brothers both,
here must you rest, remain, fulfill.

Blow gentle winds, blow gentle if you please.
Let God's own rainbow mark this quiet spot
where history in innocence forgot
to save their lives, to live in peace.

51

Mother Volga

(excerpt from the novel Mother Volga)

I saw the bleeding fall leaves play their tune
along your crying river banks.
I saw you flow, your shadow's fragrant bloom,
while night passed by, the deep dark night,
and still we never touched our hands,
together kissed the starlit sky.

And when the morning rose in grief,
the horrid war gave birth
but for a moment, just, eternal peace
began to warm the scarlet earth.

Challenge

Not gold nor pleasure be the aim
but decent law and worthwhile trust.
You - working man, again,
but fight you must.

Let tidal waves of echoes roar
to get the poison off the street.
No child shall evermore
taste such defeat.

Let rainstorms break; let blizzards rage;
let Hell freeze up with all its fright.
You - Foreman, spite your age,
join us to fight.

Let lightning fall and thunder roll;
let hammers ring into the night.
You - working men of all,
begin your fight.

Night of Hope

The softly frozen air clings to some silver branches
        beneath the window of our souls
as all along the sun tries, effortless, to part the missing sky
and cold and lonesome thoughts begin to linger on the hills
while summer's passed in distant flurries of the mind
along a hallowed sound that tolls
to flee inside the bosom's eager search
to lure the spirit's heights to try
another path of life's enriched circle
within the gleaming mirth
of sun drenched, warming hills.

And thus, with ever lingering awe,
        my soul has reached the windswept regions
where night and day, where warm and cold unite,
where past and present sleep
and have exalted you and crowned you, godlike spirit,
who's dwelt in angels' legions
that only love's most blessed sanctity adorns the child
that neither laughs nor weeps.

And when the coldest morning cracks the air
        and when the ravens gather not to fly
and when afar the icy glare
does rise above the clear blue stretch of wild'ring trees,
will shine a star beneath the shielding heaven
so bright and clear, so distant, scintillating high,
that all which seemed so hopeless and forgotten
will glow within each home alike a golden fleece.

Counsellor

I took the torch which you held then,
I raised it high into the sky.
The dim and dying flame again
began to spark and fly.

You did not care about your land
nor did you worship for a peace
which once had passed from hand to hand
from Flanders Fields beneath.

I lost my dreams - cling to those dead -
as golden sunlight touches Greece,
the Parthenon, the wars you had
for decency and peace.

From Walcheron, Laon, Verdun,
Avranche, the battles in the sky -
you lost - but most of all again
the torch which cannot cry.

I sang of you, I found no flaw.
I praised the tears, I shared your joy
and now I find my Canada
beneath the ruins of Troy.

Jim Vensel 07

The Solitaire

The long nights made the winter come
as days began to fade to grey
painting the purple, struggling sun
while in between the coldness froze
the summer's warming hours away.

And here we rest as time goes by,
and gaze into the wintry air;
where songbirds flew now ravens fly
in solemn rows of searching quest
how to replace the solitaire.

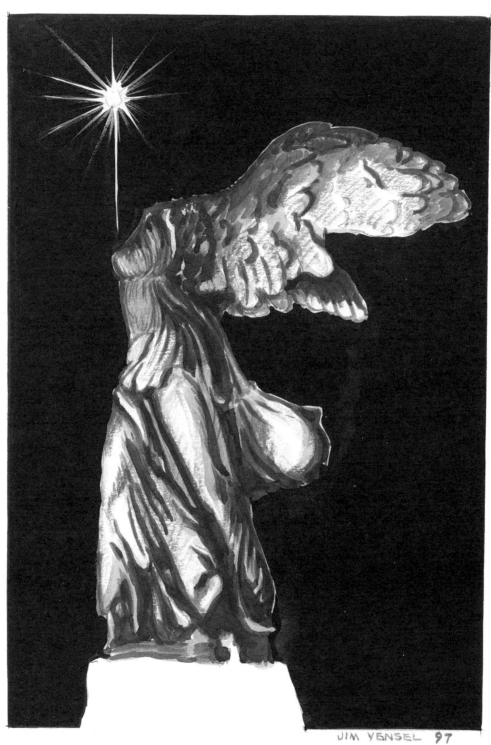

JIM VENSEL 97

The Victory?

All ye who raised the banners high above the bleeding fields,
lying somewhere amidst the longing pasture's dreaming soil,
will have to rise once more to wage the flood of hostile aim
against the ones who dare to swindle and betray and spoil,
to save all that which grieved your sacrifice when you laid claim
 to immortality which comes of age with changing yields.

Are we betrayed or are we lost or do we only fear the future dying?
Are we afraid to right the wrongs which are within our peoples' rows?
And while you fell and slipped away entrusting us to not cease trying,
we took your future and we built a paradise into the shining air
and heard the bell of glory ringing into the abyss of despair.

Once more you fallen heros, the bugle keeps on calling.
Your work was done and to remind your crosses' shadows stay.
No bell shall ring so clear into the day, night falling,
to us, what you had done but never had the time to say:
that light comes forth from darkness, shining, in spite of fear or wrath,
no sacrifice can be declining before the victory of Samothrace.

Yes, You Have Won

(Excerpt from The Lost Jade)

Which cloud is free of sunlit shadow
to keep a smile as darkness looms?
Which searching mind will leave the meadow
and make a window for its rooms?

Where falls the arrow hurled in fury
from out of thousands, into one,
the one which strikes and finds no jury;
the deed which came but was not done?

Why does the sorrow kill our laughter,
turn into foes those who were friends?
What will the hours hold thereafter
while on a path which never ends?

So drown your fears and find tomorrow
and search with courage and a smile
and learn to well go out and borrow
and give away that lonesome isle.

Just as you give away this treasure,
the one with which you could not part,
will come a million joys of pleasure,
to ever free your troubled heart.

Why is there rain and sun and thunder?
Why do we struggle on and on?
It is to know this holy wonder
when God will tell: yes, you have won.